AF409580

The Wit and Wisdom of
Wesselton Cobbler

The Wit and Wisdom of
Wesselton Cobbler

Volume 1

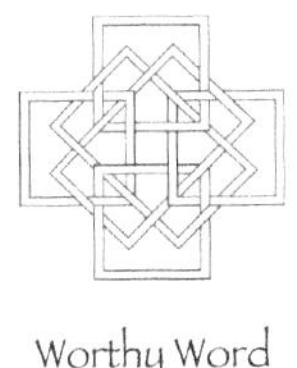

Worthy Word
Books

ISBN: 979-8-218-05637-7

Trust is everything

Give it wisely.
Earn it well.

Wesselton Cobbler

There are moments
when you must rise up
to be your own

HERO.

Wesselton Cobbler

You are not defined
by the *mistakes* you make
until you cease to learn from
them.

Wesselton Cobbler

Do not teach
your children
so much

WHERE TO GO
as
how to walk.

....

Wesselton Cobbler

grace

Accept it.
Apply it.
Pass it on.

Wesselton Cobbler

Childhood

man's great romance with life

Wesselton Cobbler

Liberty
is not
freedom from responsibility
but
freedom for responsibility.

Wesselton Cobbler

More often than not,
what is taken as an **offense**
is just uncomfortably
close to the TRUTH.

Wesselton Cobbler

Knowing how make you *useful.*

Knowing why makes you SMART.

Knowing when makes you *wise.*

Be all three.

Wesselton Cobbler

Courage

is not fearlessness
but a greater fear
of what might happen
if you do *not* act.

Wesselton Cobbler

truth
works.

Wesselton Cobbler

Maturity knows when and when not to be *immature.*

Wesselton Cobbler

Knowledge opens *possibilities.*

Wesselton Cobbler

The making of the

best *memories* is

rarely the path of

least *embarrassment*.

Wesselton Cobbler

Hold on to goodness
& it will cost you.
Hold on to evil
& it will cost everyone else.

Wesselton Cobbler

How to be Friends

Be yourself,
then trade understanding.

Wesselton Cobbler

Sacrifice seals sincerity.

Wesselton Cobbler

Theory
soothes
no pain.

Wesselton Cobbler

ACHING hearts
make
poignant pens.

Wesselton Cobbler

Mercy
for when someone can't,
not for when he won't.

Wesselton Cobbler

No *injustice*
can be righted
with another *injustice.*

Wesselton Cobbler

Folly

embraced
seals
regret.

Wesselton Cobbler

MASTER

not by force
but by understanding.

Wesselton Cobbler

Wesselton Cobbler

Irresponsibility
forfeits privilege.

Wesselton Cobbler

The masses will never be
grateful for a rescue
until they feel the
nearness of the **threat.**

Wesselton Cobbler

Difficulties

are
opportunities
to forge new connections.

Wesselton Cobbler

The hardest part about creating
is finding enough courage
to sully a pristine canvas
with the first brush stroke.

᭜᭜᭜

Wesselton Cobbler

Anxiety
deserves
to wait.

Wesselton Cobbler

*Strive more
to make memories
than* IMPRESSIONS.

Wesselton Cobbler

DUTY forges rivers.

LOVE builds bridges.

Wesselton Cobbler

Serve **rich fare**
in small portions.

Wesselton Cobbler

Dignity

Expect it.
Uphold it.
Defend it.

Wesselton Cobbler

Uncommon *intimacy*
requires
uncommon respect.

Wesselton Cobbler

Life is not about
PROVING
yourself but about
improving
yourself.

Wesselton Cobbler

Too many *flowers*
only make
more people
sneeze.

Wesselton Cobbler

Work

sharpens

wits.

Wesselton Cobbler

Your *disposition* today
is your
legacy tomorrow.

Wesselton Cobbler

Justice before *mercy*.

Wesselton Cobbler

He who fails to listen
does not deserve to be heard.

X

Wesselton Cobbler

Faith
is what draws
God's promises
into
our reality.

Wesselton Cobbler

The joys of freedom
do not come without
the **burdens**
of responsibility.

Wesselton Cobbler

Strong principles
must guard
weak resolve.

Wesselton Cobbler

Love without desire
is but labor.
Love without duty
is but lust.

Wesselton Cobbler

Climbing out of

pits

is as insurmountable as
scaling

mountains,

just without the glory.

———

Wesselton Cobbler

The first step
on a long journey
is the willingness
to take the journey.

Wesselton Cobbler

Live life as an

adventure

not as a

☑ CHECKLIST.

Wesselton Cobbler

Small is the vessel
that reaches
deep
into the well.

Wesselton Cobbler

Faith is the kind of *imagination* that is guaranteed by God.

Wesselton Cobbler

Temptation
is the
alluring garb
of regret.

Wesselton Cobbler

JUSTICE to he who
demands *mercy*;
mercy to he who
humbly accepts JUSTICE.

Wesselton Cobbler

A neighbor may
overlook your faults,
but a true friend
faces them.

Wesselton Cobbler

Critical hearts
need
willing hands.

Wesselton Cobbler

If you do not spend the **tangible**
to preserve the intangible,
you will lose them *both*.

Wesselton Cobbler

An **apology** is better than an **excuse**.

Wesselton Cobbler

Justice secures;
mercy endears.

Justice first.

———

Wesselton Cobbler

Pity the flightless birds,
but not so much
as to let them
clip your *wings*.

Wesselton Cobbler

INTEGRITY
costs
popularity.

Wesselton Cobbler

It doesn't matter so much where you start as where you're headed.

Wesselton Cobbler

I don't want you to show me
how good you are
so I can ask you why.
I want you to show me
how good God is
so I can ask you how you know.

Wesselton Cobbler

Better to be *good* & not GREAT

than GREAT & not *good*.

Wesselton Cobbler

There is no GREAT man
without a GREAT struggle.

Wesselton Cobbler

No injustice is entitled to silence.

Wesselton Cobbler

Childhood

is encountering life
as a discovery rather than
a responsibility.

Wesselton Cobbler

Honey
TAKETH AWAY

NO HUNGER.

Wesselton Cobbler

Life's goal isn't *ease*,

it's *excellence*.

Wesselton Cobbler

The good often
suffer in *silence*
where lesser men
complain.

Wesselton Cobbler

The truly GREAT men
are not those who seek greatness
but those who seek TRUTH.

ᎧᏬᎧ

Wesselton Cobbler

God is your Master,
not because He wants to control you
but because you are to be His

masterpiece.

Wesselton Cobbler

Blame the *wind*
for the *waves* ~
though without it,
you would not sail at all.

Wesselton Cobbler

Tact is hitting the nail on the head without hammering anyone's thumb.

Wesselton Cobbler

Confusion is contagious.

Wesselton Cobbler

Wisdom kept silent is worthless.

Wesselton Cobbler

waves

keep the oceans
from becoming
stagnant.

Wesselton Cobbler

exaggeration necessitates *exaggeration*

Wesselton Cobbler

Only after the blossom has died

can the sweetness of the fruit

begin to grow.

✸✸✸

Wesselton Cobbler

Friendship is
openness,
not agreement.

Wesselton Cobbler

Tragedy

knows

no words.

Wesselton Cobbler

Humbled pride
is worth
wasted resources.

Wesselton Cobbler

Beauty
lies in
imperfection.

Wesselton Cobbler

Líve,
not do.

Wesselton Cobbler

There is a depth of goodness
which only marks those
who have been through hell.

Wesselton Cobbler

LABOR
sweetens
leisure.

Wesselton Cobbler

$Love$ lies not
in the intensity of emotion
but in the intensity of devotion.

Wesselton Cobbler

Say more,
speak less.

Wesselton Cobbler

He who is hasty in JUDGMENT is soon left alone.

Wesselton Cobbler

Man does to get done.
God does to get man.

Wesselton Cobbler

An *opinion*
is of little value
if it is given
without respect.

Wesselton Cobbler

Reach for your
dreams,
temper your
appetites.

Wesselton Cobbler

"Congratulations"
is what you say
when it's too late to issue warning
and too early to offer sympathy.

Wesselton Cobbler

QUAINTNESS

is the fruit of worthy labors
after the sweat has dried.

Wesselton Cobbler

The easiest fish
to catch
are rarely
the easiest to *swallow*.

Wesselton Cobbler

An **offense**
once is a misunderstanding;
twice, a weakness;
three times, a call to action.

Wesselton Cobbler

There are **miseries**
too **deep** to be forgotten ~
they must be understood.

———

Wesselton Cobbler

Implication

speaks more POINTEDLY than denunciation.

Wesselton Cobbler

Education

---

less a filling of minds
than an opening of them

Wesselton Cobbler

BELIEF becomes *faith*
at the point of
desperation.

Wesselton Cobbler

Undisputed authority never led any man to **GREATNESS**, only to infamy.

Wesselton Cobbler

Bad manners

SPOIL GOOD EFFORT.

Wesselton Cobbler

Sorrow
is a fountain
of quiet wisdom.

Wesselton Cobbler

Guilty minds
suspect much.

Wesselton Cobbler

GREAT MEN
rise to
unheeded
goodness.

Wesselton Cobbler

A nation that fails to demand
self-restraint of its citizens
has no defense at all.

Wesselton Cobbler

In small doses,

FRANKNESS

endears.

Wesselton Cobbler

Other people notice
more than you think they do,
and most certainly
what you wish they *wouldn't*.

Wesselton Cobbler

A smile is the oil
in the machinery of life.

Wesselton Cobbler

A lash of the tongue
can sting more sharply
than the lash of a whip.

Wesselton Cobbler

Excuses

ARE THE MOST

TEDIOUS

OF ALL TALES.

Wesselton Cobbler

Trials are sent to prove

or improve a man.

PERSEVERE.

Wesselton Cobbler

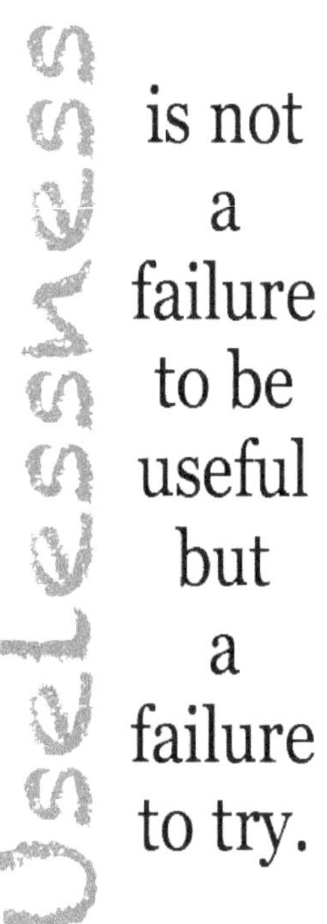

Wesselton Cobbler

Yield
no thought
to that which
deserves none.

———

Wesselton Cobbler

Wisdom seems madness
to the minds of fools.

Wesselton Cobbler

Wesselton Cobbler

The difference between
an *invitation* and an OBLIGATION
is your ability to
decline without guilt.

———

Wesselton Cobbler

The stronger man doesn't finish a needless fight, he ends it.

Wesselton Cobbler

Art is man's means
of capturing
his passions.

Wesselton Cobbler

Sow not,
reap naught.

□ □ □

Wesselton Cobbler

Conform
enough to secure.
Express
enough to connect.

Wesselton Cobbler

SPEAK NOT
of what you
KNOW NOTHING.

———

Wesselton Cobbler

He who **criticizes**
most freely
is generally
most guilty.

Wesselton Cobbler

Motivation

means

everything.

Wesselton Cobbler

CONFIDENCE
comes with just
the right blend of
success
and
failure.

———

Wesselton Cobbler

Suffering

that does

not bring

death

leaves

depth.

Wesselton Cobbler

He who **envisions** is
nothing
until he too puts
his *hands* to the plow.

—

Wesselton Cobbler

The only *hope*
for genuine / change
lies in FACING
the ugly truth.

Wesselton Cobbler

Divisions

divulge

devotion.

Wesselton Cobbler

Character

rejects an inferior comfort
to reach for a deeper reality.

Wesselton Cobbler

Oppression:

When the comfort of one costs the dignity of another.

Wesselton Cobbler

Shifting morality from OBJECTIVE to *subjective* standards is to unravel the fabric of society.

Wesselton Cobbler

Anyone who does not value *innocent* lives, ultimately, will not value more *guilty* ones either.

Wesselton Cobbler

Books

are the original

time machines.

Wesselton Cobbler

Wisdom
is what is gained
when all else is lost.

———

Wesselton Cobbler

Wesselton Cobbler

Idle hands
make weak hearts.

Wesselton Cobbler

Brokenness lends **boldness.**

Wesselton Cobbler

Goodness

shines BRIGHTEST

in the **strain**.

Wesselton Cobbler

Honor

bestowed on a **fool**

is quickly undone.

Wesselton Cobbler

Generosity
to the
generous
multiplies
virtue.

Wesselton Cobbler

The
  observations
      of the innocent
can be more **POTENT** than
  the
      eloquence
          of the wise.

Wesselton Cobbler

Familiarity lends
a superficial appearance
of worthiness.

Wesselton Cobbler

Open hearts
open hearts.

Wesselton Cobbler

A tree is not known
by its **foliage**
but by its FRUIT.

Wesselton Cobbler

What you learn today
may open the
door of opportunity
tomorrow.

————————————

Wesselton Cobbler

A little *joy*
is worth
a little **indignity**.

* * *

Wesselton Cobbler

Folly is better prevented than repaired.

Wesselton Cobbler

Why is it that those with the least to say take the longest time saying it?

Wesselton Cobbler

WISDOM is a soft whisper which is made more audible by regret.

Wesselton Cobbler

One *injustice* ignored

threatens

all JUSTICE everywhere.

❦ ❦

Wesselton Cobbler

BE GOOD *with style*.

Wesselton Cobbler

Vision

is the collision of

imagination

and

REALITY.

Wesselton Cobbler

Fear looks around.

Hope looks up.

Wesselton Cobbler

Kindness
is the most
palatable wisdom.

Wesselton Cobbler

Regret

just enough to change.

Wesselton Cobbler

A MUSCLE,
a mind,

or

a *heart*,
left un-stretched,
has forgotten how to **live**.

Wesselton Cobbler

In giving, *inspire.*
In accepting, embrace.

Wesselton Cobbler

Music flows to depths
that words fail to reach.

Wesselton Cobbler

Life

is in the **depth**

of your encounters.

Wesselton Cobbler

Foolishness deserves
no attention,
but never show **evil**
so much tolerance.

—

Wesselton Cobbler

The **best** efforts of
one *good* man
can never counteract
the devastation
caused by one madman,
but he can raise up
an army to stop him.

Wesselton Cobbler

Love opens the door
for someone else
to touch your heart.

Wesselton Cobbler

Satire

is man's consolation
for his helplessness
in the face of
unchecked injustice.

Wesselton Cobbler

Loyalty

has **NO** obligation

to *cruelty.*

Wesselton Cobbler

HAVE NO PATIENCE WITH EVIL.

Wesselton Cobbler

Sometimes
it's more efficient
to be less efficient.

Wesselton Cobbler

A speck of light
in the **darkness**
is *hope.*

A spot of **darkness**
in the light
is reality.

———

Wesselton Cobbler

Small virtues
do not excuse
great vice.

Wesselton Cobbler

Advice is
a convenient gift,
for the recipient
bears all the cost.

Wesselton Cobbler

DELEGATE RESPONSIBILITY BUT NEVER DUTY.

Wesselton Cobbler

A *good* man
will imitate a **noble** man.
A **bad** one
will counterfeit him.

Wesselton Cobbler

Life is for *living,* not just ENDURING.

Wesselton Cobbler

If we are wise,
we will heed **wisdom**.

If we are not,
we must heed **want**.

———

Wesselton Cobbler

Rights are *universal*.

Privileges are for the DUTIFUL.

Wesselton Cobbler

The audacity of evil
is *inconceivable,*
until it touches **you**.

Wesselton Cobbler

Tolerance of **immorality**
breeds
intolerance for MORALITY.

Wesselton Cobbler

If CHANGE is in
deviating from the norm,
then **chaos** is in discarding it.

Wesselton Cobbler

HARD BOUNDARIES create safe havens for *soft hearts.*

Wesselton Cobbler

CRISES

DIVULGE

CHARACTER.

Wesselton Cobbler

Family
is defined by *love*,
not **LINEAGE**.

Wesselton Cobbler

It isn't your mistakes
that are **shameful**
so much as
your **refusal**
to learn from them.

Wesselton Cobbler

Maturity

finds a way to express itself

without destroying needful order.

Wesselton Cobbler

The greatest prospect

evil has to succeed

is to go undetected.

Wesselton Cobbler

Your liberties are **sacred**, though not IRREVOCABLE. In forfeiting another's, you forfeit your own.

❖ ❖ ❖

Wesselton Cobbler

Do not trade a greater good,
however   ,
for a lesser one,
however seemingly NECESSARY.

Wesselton Cobbler

ARROGANCE invariably erupts into **shame**.

Wesselton Cobbler

Often the squeakiest wheel
is not the *neediest* one
but the greediest one.

Wesselton Cobbler

The *noble* and the *ignoble*

are most easily distinguished

by how they handle INJUSTICE.

———

Wesselton Cobbler

REALITY

is

founded

on

FACTS,

not

feelings.

Wesselton Cobbler

Love is less in the **BIG** things than in the thousand little ones.

Wesselton Cobbler

IGNORANCE

INVITES

INVASION.

———
———

Wesselton Cobbler

The gulf between
opening a book
&
opening a mind
is bridged by
opening a heart.

Wesselton Cobbler

ONE VOICE SPEAKING OUT FOR JUSTICE
IS A BLOW TO INJUSTICE EVERYWHERE.

ONE VOICE SILENCED BY INJUSTICE
IS A BLOW TO JUSTICE EVERYWHERE.

TAKE A STAND.

Wesselton Cobbler

Science speaks a TRUTH man would do well to heed.

Wesselton Cobbler

Subjectivity must
submit to objectivity
or **chaos** reigns.

Wesselton Cobbler

Inferiority was never conquered
by destroying the **threat** without
but by overcoming the **fear** within.

Wesselton Cobbler

Reason above rhetoric.

Wesselton Cobbler

Effort
may move the mountains.

Eloquence
may move the mind.

But it is

gentleness

which moves the will.

Wesselton Cobbler

There is no democracy without
individual integrity.

Wesselton Cobbler

Peace
powers progress.

Wesselton Cobbler

Greater ability
opens
greater opportunity.

Wesselton Cobbler

The **parasitic** nature of lies
requires them to have a host
who believes them.

TRUTH needs no one.

———

Wesselton Cobbler

Respect for others
begins with
respect for
yourself.

≈

Wesselton Cobbler

Gentle spirits
have known
great **sacrifice**.

Wesselton Cobbler

Live life with *expectancy,*

not expectations.

Wesselton Cobbler

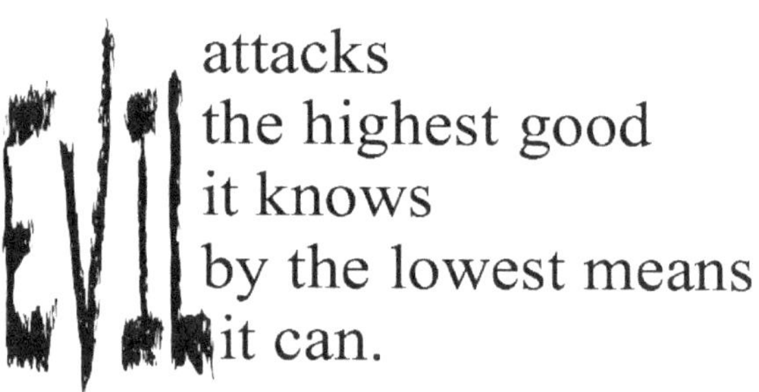

Wesselton Cobbler

Unconditional love is
not unconditional tolerance.
Love tells the truth:
God has boundaries.

Wesselton Cobbler

Stop
lingering
&
start
living.

Wesselton Cobbler

Embrace life

Enjoy life

Enrich life

Wesselton Cobbler

When loyalty
is valued over truth,
it is the innocent
who suffer.

———

Wesselton Cobbler

A truth questioned, engages.
A lie questioned, enrages.

Wesselton Cobbler

It is not ours to reconcile distortions with REALITY but to expose them as **LIES**.

Wesselton Cobbler

Unrelenting difficulties
may deplete strength,
but undisturbed ease
depletes character.

Wesselton Cobbler

THE MOST

THAT LIES CAN HAVE

IS INFLUENCE.

TRUTH HOLDS THE SUBSTANCE.

Wesselton Cobbler

There is no *hope* except that which is grounded in TRUTH.

Wesselton Cobbler

Childhood
is the greatest expedition
of DISCOVERY & adventure
any man has ever had.

Wesselton Cobbler

If JUSTICE is not served,
then *injustices*
invariably are.

Wesselton Cobbler

Dignity is a RIGHT.
Respect is a privilege.

Expect one;
earn the other.

———

Wesselton Cobbler

Even if no one else does,

TREAT YOURSELF WITH DIGNITY.

Wesselton Cobbler

All men may be created equal,
but their opinions certainly aren't!

Wesselton Cobbler

Scorched dignity

is a slow wound to heal.

Wesselton Cobbler

We do not begin to learn
until we have faced our
failures as failures.

Wesselton Cobbler

Your character
is only as strong
as what it has
cost you to keep it.

Wesselton Cobbler

When the present is consuming,
the future feels irrelevant.

Wesselton Cobbler

Ultimately, failure is not in the absence of SUCCESS but in the compromise of one's character.

Wesselton Cobbler

Goodness is grateful
where evil is insatiable.

Wesselton Cobbler

Chaos

begets

chaos.

Wesselton Cobbler

Why is it that
those most demanding of
their RIGHTS
are usually those who have
most thoroughly disregarded
their RESPONSIBILITIES?

⬚ ⬚ ⬚ ⬚

Wesselton Cobbler

Nothing closes a mind
more quickly than
comfortable ignorance.

Wesselton Cobbler

Love draws.

FEAR DRIVES.

————

Know the difference.

Wesselton Cobbler

GREATNESS

is bestowed

on DILIGENCE,

not on *dreams*.

Wesselton Cobbler

Be the kind of man
that the kind of woman you want
deserves.

Wesselton Cobbler

FIGHT FOR THE GOOD,
even if you are losing.

Wesselton Cobbler

The supreme trials of life drive you
to either cling *desperately* to goodness
or *entirely* discard it as a sham.

Time will prove your choice.

Wesselton Cobbler

A *hard road* grows easier
as the vision of the end
grows CLEARER.

Wesselton Cobbler

Success is *sweetened*

only by the failures

that proceeded it.

———————

———

Wesselton Cobbler

Any man can be critical,
but it takes a GREAT one to be critical
without becoming hypocritical.

Wesselton Cobbler

The most precious treasures

are those that you must

work *to uncover.*

Wesselton Cobbler

Require me to remember
& I will forget.
Invite me to understand
& I will remember.

Wesselton Cobbler

Goodness shines most clearly

in the midst of **deep darkness**~

though for the star,

there may be no light.

Wesselton Cobbler

Take refuge in the **truth**,
for any lies you hide behind
will eventually betray you.

Wesselton Cobbler

At the end of the day,

the one who remains is

not he who **fought** the
hardest
but he who **STOOD** the
strongest.

Wesselton Cobbler

Accepting the TRUTH

is the first step towards *hope*.

Wesselton Cobbler

Romance

is in the tentative anticipation.

Wesselton Cobbler

A man will never be able
to stand alone
until he has learned
to walk alone.

Wesselton Cobbler

The truest hearts are often also the most timid.

Wesselton Cobbler

Normal
is overrated.

Wesselton Cobbler

Strive less
to be **admired** than
to find reasons
to **admire** others.

Wesselton Cobbler

Truth needs but few words.

Wesselton Cobbler

The best way to be

loved extravagantly

is to

love extravagantly.

Wesselton Cobbler

Hold to integrity.
Fools will try to *persuade* you
to compromise it.
The wicked will try to **master** you
because of it.
Stand for right anyway.

Wesselton Cobbler

Love may break the heart,
but it is
hate which breaks the *spirit*.

Wesselton Cobbler

Real heroes
don't wear
capes;
they wear
scars.

Wesselton Cobbler

Science is only as RELIABLE

as the people representing it.

Wesselton Cobbler

A wrong contemplated
needs VIGILANCE.
A wrong in progress
needs JUSTICE.
A wrong completed
needs redemption.

Respond appropriately.

Wesselton Cobbler

Tempered passion

burns truest.

——•——

Wesselton Cobbler

Why is it that those who
demand respect the most
usually *deserve* it the least?

Wesselton Cobbler

Hope fuels *passion.*

Wesselton Cobbler

Somewhere between
the **laxness** of comfort
& the **agony** of despair
lies the motivation to
reach beyond *mediocrity*.

Wesselton Cobbler

Love fills in for
the little deeds
that **DUTY** leaves
undone.

Wesselton Cobbler

SUCCESS may be measured
by the reception of the product,
but *satisfaction* is measured
by the richness of the process.

Wesselton Cobbler

Talk cheapens
the *deepest* communion.

Wesselton Cobbler

Our greatest **strengths**
become
our greatest weaknesses
when they are serving
the wrong ends.

Wesselton Cobbler

Promises lightly made are lightly broken.

Wesselton Cobbler

Compromise your integrity
for no man;
& require no man to
compromise his for you.

Wesselton Cobbler

An isolated sacrifice
is heroism;
if it is returned,
that is friendship.

Wesselton Cobbler

The greater your
depth of UNDERSTANDING,
the more broadly
you will be *misunderstood.*

Wesselton Cobbler

Elaborate façades hide disintegrating foundations.

Wesselton Cobbler

A humble spirit
lends quiet trust.

Wesselton Cobbler

Serving willingly

is one of life's greatest *joys*.

Serving unwillingly

is one of life's most bitter **sorrows**.

Wesselton Cobbler

Be busy
with the things
that matter,
yet at *leisure* enough
to do the things
that matter most.

Wesselton Cobbler

Keep to the purpose,
    not to the particulars.

◎◎◎

Wesselton Cobbler

Aspire
TO
inspire.

Wesselton Cobbler

The surest way of becoming either

superbly good

or

unashamedly bad

is to be treated with **injustice**.

Wesselton Cobbler

Genius

is invariably

PECULIAR.

Wesselton Cobbler

Happiness
lies somewhere
between
indulgence
&
ENDURANCE.

Wesselton Cobbler

Live simply,

& then

simply live.

Wesselton Cobbler

<u>A child's plea:</u>

Interest me much.
Engage me more.
Love me most.

Wesselton Cobbler

It is a small man indeed

who tries to achieve GREAT things

without attending to the little ones.

Wesselton Cobbler

The best people are
those who have been
purified by fire.

Wesselton Cobbler

Self-righteousness
is as **repulsive** as
genuine goodness
is *compelling*.

Wesselton Cobbler

Man will fight.
If he has no WORTHY cause,
he will find an unworthy one.

Wesselton Cobbler

FUTILE are the efforts
to explain **noble** blows
to ignorant people.

Wesselton Cobbler

Excuses rarely SATISFY anyone, except their inventor.

Wesselton Cobbler

There is a *joy* in bearing suffering that you ought which is conspicuously absent in bearing that which you ought **NOT**.

Wesselton Cobbler

Character

is in the little things
that *blossom* into

GREATNESS.

Wesselton Cobbler

A MIGHTY
FOREST
grows
in
silence.

Wesselton Cobbler

Love
does not let go so easily.

Wesselton Cobbler

PURPOSE
purges pettiness.

Wesselton Cobbler

Analysis
obliterates
intimacy.

Wesselton Cobbler

Gentleness
can move
MIGHTIER
BOULDERS
than
LEGIONS OF MEN.

Wesselton Cobbler

Silent suffering sweetens.

Wesselton Cobbler

An **advertised** virtue
is no virtue at all.

Wesselton Cobbler

Good transforms
into *goodness*
once **self-interest**
has become irrelevant.

Wesselton Cobbler

Criticism

is most **potent**

when used sparingly.

Wesselton Cobbler

Memories

are the shadow

of a life set aloft.

Wesselton Cobbler

Desperation

dissolves

diffidence.

Wesselton Cobbler

The more you realize
how much God believes in *you,*
the easier it is to believe in *Him.*

———

Wesselton Cobbler

In the
shattered
mess
of regret
lies the **hope**
of a lesson learned.

Wesselton Cobbler

Love,
without its object,
aches.

Wesselton Cobbler

Perfection constrains *imagination.*

Wesselton Cobbler

Such
profound statements
ought to be
ignored.

Wesselton Cobbler

* 9 7 9 8 2 1 8 0 5 6 3 7 7 *